Broken to Peace

NeeJay Sherman

Disclaimer

The purpose of this book is to enlighten and educate and reflect on the purpose and reality of life. This work of author is a reflection of some of her real-life events and experiences. Any resemblance with a person will be a mere coincidence.

Legal Notice:

NeeJayShermanM1@gmail.com

Acknowledgment

✧

To those
finding peace
within their broken pieces;
I'm rooting for you.
I believe in you.
You shall find it
one day!

✦✧✦

Epilogue

✧

Over the years, I have come to realize one basic principle about life: things don't always go the way we plan or occur at the time we want them to happen.

This uncertainty and oblivion bring us our fair share of struggles, often when we're least prepared for them. However, believe that these struggles are blessings in disguise.

Embrace them, and you'll start to understand the purpose they serve. There is always an underlying reason as to why certain things turn out the way they do. You *will* gain wisdom, hope, strength, and faith that the Lord has written for you.

You will come out stronger and wiser.

Have faith.

Hold on!

To my *Mommy*
I miss you more than anything in this world.
I've been all shattered and lost ever since you passed.
It's been three years now since you moved on, and my heart still aches as if it was yesterday.
I'm not the same person I used to be. I'll never be the same without you.
Your bright smile, your contagious laughter, your warm hugs, and your messages of wisdom and encouragement – I miss everything about you!
Not a day goes by where you don't cross my mind. You were the best mother to us. In the whole wide world.
Your genuinely caring nature, selflessness, kindness, and loving heart is something everyone could look up to.
Alas! You're gone.

I cannot thank you enough for all that you taught me, and the endless sacrifices you made for me. I am truly blessed to have had an angel for a mother.
I love you today and I'll love you forever.
Here's to hoping that we meet again...

*"**The Lord is close to the brokenhearted** and saves those who are crushed in spirit."— Psalm 34:18*

Chapter 1:

Love

All my life,
I have heard everybody say
love hurts...
but that is not true...
it's not love, but
the loneliness,
the rejection, and
losing someone
near and dear to your heart
that hurts,
and leaves a void,
never to be filled!
You're never the same again.

Often, we tend to get loneliness, rejection, and loss confused with love—but in reality, love is the only thing in this world that covers up all the pain. Love is the only thing in this world that does not hurt. Love is the ultimate cure for all wounds and scars!

Love Whilst You Can

Love whilst you can, for time, is only ever now—
the future does not yet exist,
so allow yourself the time
to be with those you love and admire;
to be present in stillness, in connection—
with something deep and profound!

There is a higher power,
so don't let yourself be overcome
by emotion, or by negativity,
ill wishes, evil thoughts, or anything short of devotion.
Dedicate your time and energy
to your friends and family,
for the people in your life are
genuinely your alchemy.

So, what is life without love?
In truth, there is nothing else—
for all that exists is a gift from above.
God, source, spirit, the universe, or the goddess—
are all equal in His eyes,
All that matters is that you are honest.
with yourself, with the world,
and with those
who mean the world to you!

Be honest with yourself—
do you really have time for anything less?
Any thought or feeling that does not
connect you to someone else
simply no longer serves you,
and you know this to be true.

All the answers are within... you, and only you!
Unconditional love is the ultimate rule.

"You gotta dance like there's nobody watching,
Love like you'll never be hurt,
Sing like there's nobody listening,
And live like it's heaven on earth."

— William W. Purkey

Reflections on Loneliness and Loss

I'm flawed, but
my heart is pure,
and the love I give is real.
Despite the distance between us, I can feel
your heart right next to mine.
We are one
in body, spirit, and mind.

Loneliness comes
as part and parcel with life,
and I have come to realize this now—
that to be alone is to be *all one;*
there is wisdom in your solitude.

Can you love without loss?
Isn't loss an inevitable part of life?
I believe it is, but
it has taken me a long time to realize.
Yet, here I am... Still so young—
With my whole life ahead of me,
And no idea where the winds of time will take me!
.

"The loneliest moment in someone's life is when they are watching their whole world fall apart, and all they can do is stare blankly."

— F. Scott Fitzgerald

Thank you!
Thank you for showing me what love is.
Thank you for the care and love that you've given me, and—
for being the only one who understood me.
You were an essential part of my life—and for this, I am grateful.
You are still someone special—you will be, forever!

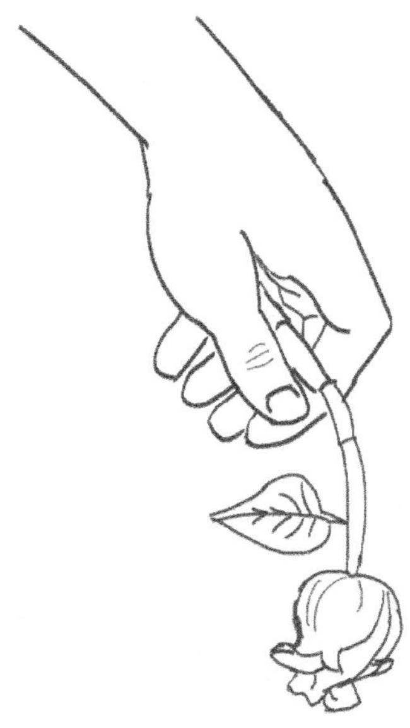

To Be Loved with All Your Flaws

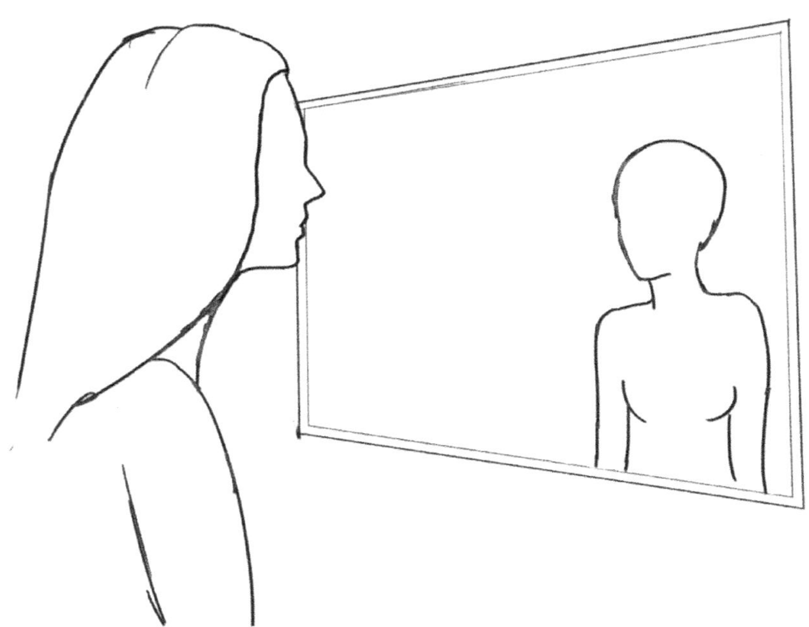

What a beautiful feeling it is,
to be loved for who you are.
For all your flaws, with all your scars,
For the light that you carry around.

A love like that, makes you feel
as if you are flying when you actually fall.
But life is uncertain, and the road has bumps
there are ups and downs, and mundane routines
days spiral into the night, and night into day
and from the darkness rises, the sun,
in all its majestic glory!

Life is a beautiful thing, yet a mystery—
We are perfectly imperfect,
and attempting to carry on
with dignity; yet
a loss is real,
and love often fades,
and the darkness and light within
both exist in synergy—
in perfect harmony beneath the skin.
And my flaws—those real things
that make me, ME!
that make me feel
like I can't be loved,
or that I'm inherently broken—aren't even real.
When you find those people, who love you for who you are,
hold onto them with all your might
love, with all your heart
Be real, be true
Be YOU

"I'm selfish, impatient and a little insecure. I make mistakes, I am out of control and at times hard to handle. But if you can't handle me at my worst, then you sure as hell don't deserve me at my best."

— Marilyn Monroe

You deserve more than a half-hearted love.
You are complete, and so is your love,
Do not settle for anything less.
Hold onto the ones you love, because
the best ones don't come twice.

If you love someone, pray for them.
Pray for their *peace.*
Pray for their *growth.*
Pray for their *success.*
Pray for their *happiness.*

Maybe the most significant plot twist
we are all waiting for
is 'self-love.'
Let's love and *forgive ourselves.*
Let's congratulate ourselves on a job well done.
Things may have gone the wrong way, but
it sure taught us all a lesson.
Your loved ones may leave,
but their memories are forever!

The Cyclic Nature of Love

I know, someday,
all the love that you give
will come back to you...
Love is cyclic—you receive what you offer.
People often say
That suffering and loss are avoidable.
If you don't love.
Yet I don't believe that's true.
They are both fundamental parts of life;
Without them, we would not know
Love, joy and light.

Darkness is within all of us
and everything—within every cell,
every atom; darkness is a seed for light to grow...
Yet it is also emptiness, loss, and grief
and from the ashes, rises a new creation.

And so, it spirals round and round...
love, light, darkness, loss, unity, separation—
there's a connection.

It's all an illusion, like they say
But deep down, I also know, that
Someday all the love that you give will come back to you...

You are *worth it.*
You are *important.*
You are *beautiful.*
You are *loved.*
You're going to spend
your nights searching

for what we had
in other people, but
you will never find it;
because no one will love you as I did.

✧✦

The Ache of Love thats Lost

How can I move on?
How can I get over?
When I'm still in love with you?

You were the first person,
I fell in love with.
You showed me what love really felt like,
but you were also my biggest heartbreak... Oh, the irony!

When you love someone, you feel it
deep in your heart and gut.
You feel it in your bones. In your veins, and skin.

I got addicted to you so quickly.
And now that you're gone, I don't know
What to do with my life!

"Just because you have a past with someone, doesn't mean you should have a future with them."

-Robert Tew

Love makes you lose your
Mind A Little...

Love makes you lose your mind a little,
like your inner crazy comes out to say,
"hey—let's get into this mess!"
You feel deeply
because
your real mind comes out of tune;
the thoughts in your mind,
and the emotions you feel
don't represent
the real you!

To be in love
is a beautiful thing.
It's the type of feeling
and emotion
that makes your soul sing,
and your spirit shines—
like no others'—
as being in love is madness;
the epiphany of being human—
the coexistence of bliss and sadness.

Because to love is to lose,
and to lose is to win,
Two parallel cycles
within the same spin.
Life is a game, a crazy game indeed—
but a game after all,
and like all games,

you either win or lose,
and even losing has its blessings,
lessons in healing,
forgiveness, and blame...
There is sanity in insanity,
and a light in the dark.

"Don't dwell on what went wrong. Instead, focus on what to do next. Spend your energies on moving forward toward finding the answer."
-Denis Waitley

"This generation has lost the value of love, the value of trust, and the value of communication."

Personal Reflections

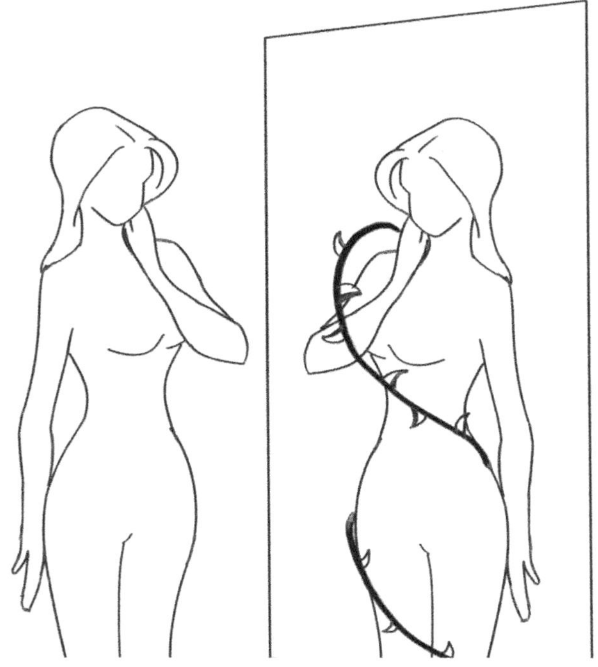

I keep having flashbacks,
Of the time we spent together.
All the memories fill my head,
good and bad...
all that you taught me about love and myself,
I thank you for that.
If ever I said,
Something rude or bad,
In anger or despair,
that made you love me a little less.
I regret it now. I take it back.

When I love, I love deep—
so, when I'm hurt, I'm hurt deep.
I know for a fact
That I gave you
the purest form of love you had ever received...
and I am honored.

Your first love will always be
your truest love.
You can't ever love
like that again.
Spend your whole life
looking for that person
in everyone else...

When you find
someone worthy in this world,
hold onto them—
with love.
Not desperation.

You need someone who goes out of their way to make it evident that they want you in their life.

✧

"In the end, my love for you is still pure and genuine."

The Story of Blue Jay

After my mother passed, we started experiencing a lot of spiritual activities at home.

A few days
after she set off
on her next journey,
I was asleep alone.
In the same room we shared,
just before she departed.
I felt someone's presence,
warm and kind,
rubbing my head
and leaving my heart,
all warm, and content.

My mother used to rub my head—
Just like that!
I knew it was her,
And I dozed off,
In peace!

Then, when I opened my eyes,
I saw someone
walk out of my room.
Yet there was no one there—
just a presence,
a strong but silent guiding light...
So despite my initial jumpiness,
surprise, and
self-questioning—
I chose love over fear and fright.
For I knew it was her,
My dear mother!

Look, girl!
Life is not restricted
to this one incarnation,
there is indeed life after death!
A new cycle begins when
we say goodbye to the flesh
and lay our loved ones
to rest!

This is the beauty
of losing someone you love.
It can help you see
the nature of spirit and existence—
And how love is all there truly is...
We all are connected through
divine assistance.

***

My mom's middle name is
BlouJay, pronounced *bluejay,*
Though she's long gone, she still comes
and shows us
she has found her peace—
even to this day!
Blue Jays and Red Cardinals
started to fly
past our house
in the backyard,
making sure they were never away
too long and never went too far.

And then once time,

my sister was sad,
so she went
for a nature walk;
right there in front of her,
as if placed as a message,
there was a blue jay feather!

Angels are real,
and so are spirits—
always reassuring
we are protected
and cherished—
We both knew that day
that our mom was letting us know
she was with us!

They often say
children can see things we can't—
their minds are still in tune with the veil!
I now believe that's true!

My four-year-old nephew once said
something which proved
how spirit's powers never fail.
It was night, and
my sister was reading him
a story for bedtime;
And right there,
in the corner of the room was
my mom—
silently present,
supportive... divine!

"In my experience, self-hatred is the dominant malaise crippling Christians and stifling their growth in the Holy Spirit."

— Brennan Manning

Chapter 2: Loss

What's more heartbreaking than losing the love of your life?
"Losing them twice."

Spirals

You smile, but
you want to cry.
You talk,
yet you're quiet inside.
You pretend like you're happy, but you aren't.
You want to be strong,
but you can't.

You're breaking down.
Losing it all.
And there's nothing you could do about it.

That heartbreak that you can physically feel...
when your chest gets really tight,
ribs closing in on your heart,
suffocating you,
you find yourself struggling to breathe,
and it doesn't feel real.
It feels as if life itself is a big bad joke,
and each time you try to express it—
all you can do is choke!

On your own tears...
your heart.
The reality which was once true
is gone,
like the spirals
that connect me to you.

"Modern man must descend the spiral of his own absurdity to the lowest point; only then can he look beyond it. It is obviously impossible to get around it, jump over it, or simply avoid it."

-Vaclav Havel

Out of the Zone

On days like today,
where I feel lost
and out of my zone,
I repeat to myself
that it's fine
to be alone.
It's okay not to be okay,
and it's alright to feel—
There's beauty in the emptiness,
as it makes me feel real.

Life is not all sunshine and rainbows,
Or calm winds and clear skies—
It is also filled with hurricanes, lightning
and demise.
There is not just white and gold,
but black is a color too—
And gray, brown, and all dark shades
cannot go unused.

There is surreal beauty
in the emptiness
and wisdom only brought by loss,
I learn to love my shadow,
low moods, and failures.
When you think you're winning,
life will always come up a twist—
Bringing darkness and destruction,
Grief and loss,
which will overshadow your bliss.

See, girl!

It is okay not to be okay;
Please do not feel sad or low—
And please don't attempt to prevent
this natural process flow.
For this is but a phase, a rather dark and gloomy one,
And it will take some time to pass.
I have come to realize
that love and life both
involve loss,
and that my heart will still keep beating,
just like Christ's did on the Cross.

I will never understand the hurt and the devastation around us and why tragedy strikes so suddenly, when you're least prepare to cope with it. But I also trust in God's perfect plan and loving nature through all of it.

It is sturdy and messy, but it's called having faith. And it's in these testing times, that you realize how firm and strong is your faith in God.

You don't need to have all the answers when you know that God does. Let go of the struggle to figure everything out on your own—seek God and trust that He is leading you through the path. To eternal peace and tranquility.

Having faith in God doesn't keep you at bay from fierce battles and hard times. But it's what gets you through them. Do not try to run away from such testing times. For hiding won't subside your pain. Feel it to the core. Cry if you must. Pour your heart out. And know that God's seeing you.

Do not hide your weary heart; God feels it. Please do not hide, because He wants Himself to be there for your brokenness, for your weariness. He loves you more than you love Him, and He doesn't want you to suffer alone.

Please, have Him in there!

Trust Him and Let Him Restore Your Broken Self

What does God mean to you?
You may still believe
in a higher power,
but not read the Bible.
You may resonate with Christianity,
yet also with Buddhism, and with other religions.
Can you feel God in your heart and soul...?

Whatever belief, theology or faith,
You follow,
Know that there is Almighty Power that loves you
And will guide you
Through the labyrinth
Of grief and despair.

If you have faith,
You can feel His love.
Allow your unseen Guide
to restore and heal you.
There is excellent power in the *Spirit*.

I thank God and my parents for the way I was raised, and they made me the woman I am today. I see this generation, and it scares me. All I can do is pray, console this generation of women—and instill in my future daughters the morals, values and respect my parents taught me.

"Depression is the most painful battle. It's real, it's not a joke or some kind of drama. If you see someone fighting with it, talk to them and listen to them. Don't let them fight alone. They may look happy, but deep inside, they're suffering. Help them heal.

A big part of depression is feeling really lonely, even if you're in a room full of a million people."

-Lilly Singh

✦

Dealing with loss is something that will never get easier to handle. The heaviness and pain always serve as a reminder to love upon the people you love—don't take them for granted, and try and make peace wherever you go. Nothing is certain. Love while you can. Live while you're alive!

✦

Loss is painful.
It's a stark reminder of how short life is—
and when you lose something forever,
it is like an emptiness.
It feels like you'll never be whole again...

✦

I'm learning
that grieving is a process
and that it is okay to not be okay;
it's okay to be in a weird mental space,
to feel off-center, or sad sometimes...
It's a natural part of life,
and sometimes very appropriate.
But I'm also learning
to let it move through
because the real challenge is
not staying stuck there.

✦

Anxiety and depression
are invisible wars
that you don't know
someone is fighting.

A Short Poem on Grief

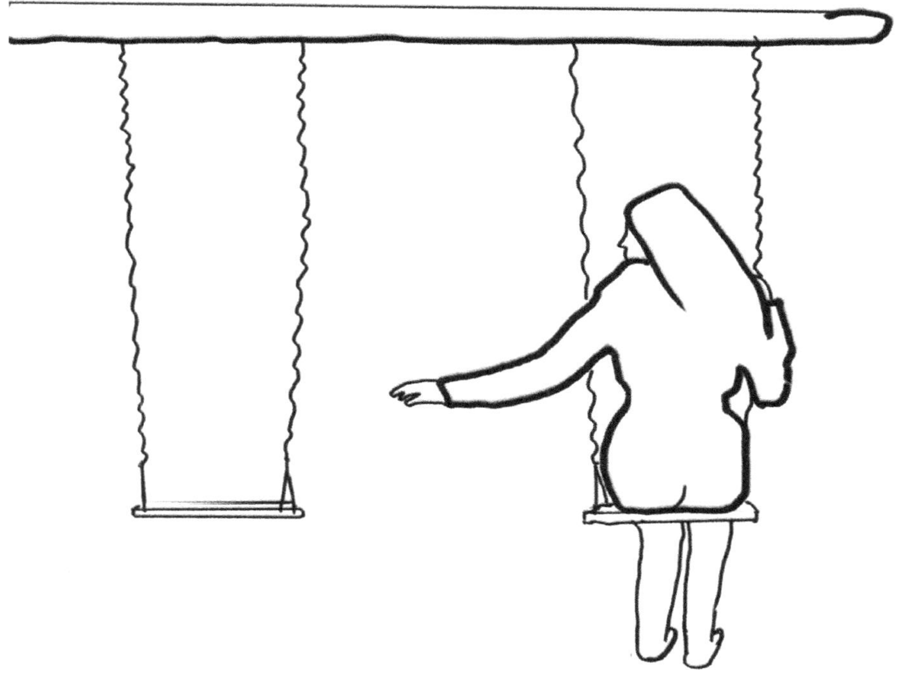

Grief: a personal and individual process.

Life is beautiful
when you stop to breathe in the air,
or when you take a moment
to be still in nature
or through prayer.

Life is divine
when you learn to harmonize your mind,
and see through a new lens,
in harmony with space and time.

See, love is all there is, in essence—
and loss is just an illusion;
space and time,
body, spirit, and mind all exist
in fusion.

Separation is a natural part of life,
a divine spiral that teaches gratitude,
so, we can connect to ourselves—
our own inner cores—
to learn our love's magnitude.

Solitude can be a blessing,
and loneliness can be beautiful,
so long as we can merge with the grief
and come out of it more dutiful—
to ourselves...

You deserve that much, don't you?

A Short Poem on Rejection

Rejection is the reason why
people deny what they really feel,
it is one of the most powerful natural forces,
that makes you feel real.
This is because rejection
gets you at your core—on a soul level;
it makes you feel and reminds you
of how much you are loveable.

To love is to be loved,
and to be loved is to love,
with the fire of a phoenix,
and the inner peace of a dove.
When you are rejected,
a piece of you breaks down inside—
And it can make you escape
to places where you shouldn't really hide.

Your love is real;
your love is pure—
your love is powerful beyond measure!
So why do you shield your heart
from life's real treasures?
Is it better to lose people
not meant for you,
and move on with pride and humility?
Or to exhaust yourself trying
to grow with people
who will never be?

With each closing and end,
there is another window or door,

even in a room with no escape—
there is still a chance for thunder,
hurricane or storm.
There will always be a space
for your heart to heal and grow;
rejection is a new beginning,
a fresh start, and new seed to sow.

So, let's ignore each other,
Try to pretend
the other person doesn't exist—
But deep down,
we both know
it wasn't supposed to end like this.

You didn't choose me...
why didn't you pick me...?
I wonder!

I stay up late at night
thinking of you,
while trying not to think about you;
missing you,
whilst trying not to miss you...

Imagine how heartbreaking it must be
to suddenly stop talking to the person
you thought you'd marry.
The worst part is letting go of all our promises,
memories, and the good times

we shared.
As hard as I try to move on and forget about you,
these memories will still stay forever in my mind.

Thanks for showing me
how love feels.
Thank you for showing me
how loss feels, too.
Thanks for making me strong
when things were falling apart.
Thank you for the try,
at least we had a good start.

With every loss, there's a gain.
Stay vulnerable, and don't drown in your thoughts.
Keep it present.

Don't worry about your troubles.
Just remember:
God will give you the strength to endure
whatever you're going through.
Right now!

If today is hard,
reminds you of loss,
or puts you in unwelcoming spaces:
please know
that I love you.
I will forever do!

"To the world you may be one person, but to one person you are the world."

– Bill Wilson

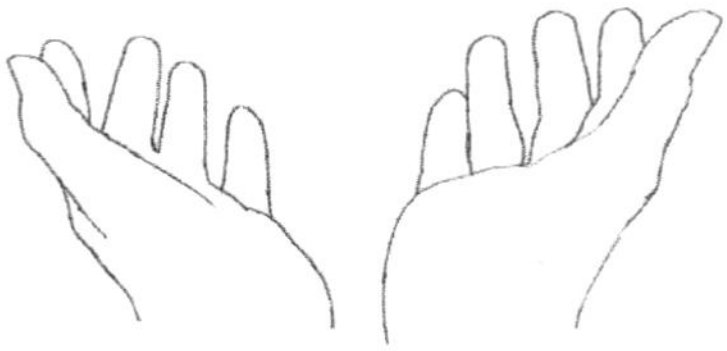

Let's pray for
Those who are about to give up.
Lord,
Give them hope.
Help them hold on.
Amen.

I miss the feeling
of you missing me.
Have you ever felt homesick,
but for a person?
There's no life without death,
no love without loss...
and that scares me.
I feel everything
so intensely and deeply.
I'm hyper empathetic.
It's been my weakness, but it's also
why I'm so *passionate*.
It's crazy how sad you can be
but still manage to smile...
how weak you can feel,
but continue to tell yourself
you're strong...
how alone you feel
in a room full of people...
how "I'm okay" continues to slide out
when you really want to break down...
Yet, don't let anyone else make you feel
as if you have to suppress your feelings,
because they cannot understand your hurt.
Emotions are important.
Feel them, accept them, then let them go.
The moment you suppress your feelings
is the moment you commit to self-abuse.
Just allow yourself to mourn
whatever it is...
Stop shaming yourself into being fake-okay
when you're not. *Feel.*

What's worse than being left?

You are near, even if I don't see you.
You're with me,
even when you're far away.
You're in my heart,
in my thoughts, in my life—
Always.

Stop breaking your own heart
for someone who isn't even fighting
to keep yours in one piece.

"The biggest loss I ever took was begging you to love me as I love you, to love me the way I deserve to be loved..."

I miss how we used to talk,
how you used to ask me
how my day was
and if I was okay.
I miss you.
I miss how things used to be.
Now we don't even talk anymore,
and it's killing me.

I lost a piece of me when you passed,
I haven't been the same ever since...
a part of me will always be with you.
I was afraid of losing you,
and that's precisely what ended up happening.
I wasn't ready to face that fear.
I wish you would visit me in my dreams.
I wish I could see you one more time.
I wish...

Life is not always great.
Often life is very hard,
but still, it goes on.

For some people, that is not as comforting of a thought as it is to others. But while it goes on, there is a joy to be found. Sometimes, it's tough to remember if it's been a long time since you've last found it.

Mind Yo-yo

Who am I?
How did I get here?
How do I escape?
Why is this happening to me?
What is the end purpose
of this game called life?
No matter what I'm doing—
in some way, shape or form,
you're always on my mind.
RIP to all the hours of sleep
I've lost to overthinking.

That broken thing that you keep trying to put back together is saving your life from that beautiful thing that's waiting to be built.

Between rain and storm,
Between day and night—
Between black and white,
Between love and hate—
Between happy and sad;
you are the first thing
that comes to my mind.

Tell me that I can live without you.
Tell me that I can face everything.
Tell me that I can still be stronger
without you.

Have you ever just sat there and thought "damn! I have been through a lot!?"

You Came to Me in a Dream...

I woke up
in the middle of the night,
around 3 am,
with water overflowing my eyes;
the purity of my love,
heartache,
and my strength
was projecting into my tears and cries.
So many nights I prayed to God,
asking if He would let my mom
visit me—once
Yet in all of my hopes,
intentions and faith,
I never conceived
we would actually meet in a dream.

In my dream, I was in a church,
standing up in the middle of a pew—
There were other people,
but I couldn't see their faces;
it didn't matter if they were people I knew,
for all that mattered was you—
the others were all black shadows;
you, dear mom, were the angel I wanted to see—
the angel I know and chose.

The timing was divine, a natural alignment,
a merging of spirit and flesh,
because between 3 and 4 in the morning
is the prime time, where the veil is thin

between life and death;
Between the dream world and waking life,
all dimensions of being...
this is the time spirit is most connected
to heart, body, mind, and seeing.

In my dream, I heard the choir singing—
yet I could not see them directly;
they were the background music
to help, assist, and aid in the connection—gently, yet intensely.
And there you were, standing on the stage,
right in the center of the spotlight—
And I knew at that moment
the soul-shaking truth:
that you had returned to pure light.

She looked at me and began to smile,
whole-heartedly waving at me;
next, she began to walk
through the pews to leave.
I began to run after her,
wanting to know where she was going,
and why—
And before she disappeared
into the infinite and unknown,
she spoke words which had never left my side.

"I'm always with you, my darling!
I never left you,"
she spoke directly to me
with a warm smile
and gleaming eyes.

Just as the shadows around me
became faces—faces of family,
loving and wise.
"*I'm always with you, I never left you*"
these words will never leave my soul,
as I know the truth within...
my mom is an angel at home.
She's still with me!

"Love takes off masks that we fear we cannot live without and know we cannot live within."

— James Baldwi

Chapter 3: Self-love

Self-Love is True Love

All of us humans,
With emotions and heart,
Are bound to fall in love,
At least once in a lifetime!
Love dawns over us,
Like early morning breeze,
And sweeps us off our feet.
Love comes to you
In more relations than one
But the best form of love you will ever fall in
Will be self-love!

Loss, grief,
And other tragedies of life
May make you love yourself a little less.
And you may find yourself
Searching for love
In other people.
You may even become
Codependent on them
Without you even realizing.
However, soon or late,
You'll come to know
How toxic it gets and
makes yourself weak.

Girl, you need to learn this by heart

People will come and they will go
Cherish when are around
Love them with all your
Heart and soul!
But, in that process,
Do not forget, sis.
You come first,
And nobody deserves your love,
More than you!

I have come to realize it now,
Spirit, God,
and life itself
provided the space
for me to be.
The parting of ways
connected me
to my own divinity.

It is easy, when in love
to begin to fall into detrimental cycles,
to get trapped
in codependency,
games, and illusions—
because life itself is constant spin and spirals.
Yet this spiral was unhealthy,
unkind, and destructive—
a knife to soul and heart.
And now, from the space
and separation,
I am healed and whole within.

When I love, I love deep—yet
self-love is the end
and the beginning.
You can't truly love another being
until you are healed and
complete within...

You glow differently when you know your value.
So now I am focused
on bettering my skin,
growing my hair,
eating well,
Taking care of my body,
Challenging my mind,
Open to abundance,
And keeping positive energy
Around me, always!

Ultimately, the person you should love the most
is you!

Zone out anything irrelevant,
and focus on yourself.
You managed to overcome
some severe heartbreak;
you have survived
the roughest disappointment;
you are strong—never forget this.

But also,
never forget
to be open for chances
of a new beginning.

Know your worth—
never sleep on yourself, sis.
When someone takes away your love—
realize that it is time
to love yourself more.

My main focus right now is mastering inner peace, and channeling my energy to become the best version of myself.
more self-love...
more self-worth...
more self-growth...
more self-improvement...
more self-control!

It's "me" time, and I think
it's not bad to treat myself
right this time.

And, I know
It's beautiful.

✧

Self-love doesn't have to be
selfish or arrogant.
It's about taking care of yourself
and giving yourself
the same amount of love
that you provide to others.

✦

Enough with putting deadlines
on your healing,
and bounding yourself
within a timeframe.
Just let it be.
Be kind to yourself,

and be patient with your process.
Be a little selfish
with your energy, and indulge in self-love
unapologetically.

✦

Every kind of relationship
eventually ends
in parting ways
or death.
Heartbreak is inevitable, but
at the end of it all,
you have to be secure enough in yourself
and believe in your own abilities.
Never give up on the things
that matter to you.

✦

It's totally okay to not to be strong.
It's okay to break.
It's okay to have a meltdown.
It's okay to fall.
It isn't a sign of weakness,
It's but only natural.
We are only human.
Cry it out, pick yourself up,
and focus on what's ahead of you.
You will make it through.

✦

I pray you quit
overthinking,
replaying failed scenarios,

feeding self-doubt,
and seeing the good
in everyone but yourself.
You deserve more.

✦

I've been apologizing
all of my life
for who I am.
For loving too deeply,
for being too sensitive, and
for being too passionate.
I'm not apologizing anymore.
I have helped people heal
while being completely broken myself.
It's time to love myself a bit more.

✦

Certain people and situations
make you look at life differently,
and make you want to change
your character.
Sometimes life puts you
in situations that make you change
not because you want to,
but because you have to.

✦

The sensitivity shouldn't be something to avoid—
it's okay to feel.

"The most important thing in life is to learn how to give out love, and to let it come in."

— Morrie Schwartz

Learn to enjoy your own company.
When you are in it,
and at genuine peace,
it can honestly be one of the best things.
I am now at a place in my life
where peace is a priority.
I deliberately avoid
certain people
to protect my mental, emotional,
and spiritual state of health.
At the end of the day,
your sanity is way more important
than anything driving you crazy—
trying to figure out
why things happened
the way they did.
It's beyond your control.
Let it go.

How you love yourself
is how you teach others
to love you.

"Life is a series of natural and spontaneous changes. Don't resist them; that only creates sorrow. Let reality be reality. Let things flow naturally forward in whatever way they like."

— Lao Tzu

✧

Personal Reflections

✦

I'm ready to leave
the hurt and the pain.
I'm prepared to leave
the tears and the sleepless nights.
I've been drowning in this pain for so long.
I've lost my identity in it.

✦

Stop chasing after people
and being the only one
trying to fix everything.
It's mentally and physically exhausting.
You have to find peace
with whoever comes and goes
from your life.
Don't be the only one putting in the effort—
you will end up losing yourself
trying to save everyone else.

✦

No matter how much it hurts now,
one day I will look back and realize
it changed my life for the better.
There was a purpose in my pain.

✦

I feel things so deep
that sometimes it can be detrimental,
and I can linger on pain forever—
which causes me to have
a negative outlook on life.
I'm always making other people happy
and not working
on my own inner happiness.
Now, I'm working on that.
I need to.

✦

I'm letting go
of all that I can't control.
I'm closing my eyes
and praying over
what is not mine to understand
or make sense of.
I'm trusting God to guide me.
I'm exhaling anxiety and fear
and allowing whatever comes to come.

✦

I'm working on
my inner and outer glow.
Time for some soul searching
and self-reflection.

✦

I learned that I love people so hard
that I can lose myself in the process.
I learned to love myself,

and only love people
who make me a better me.
I learned that God always makes a way.
You just need to trust Him!

✦

Growth is painful,
change is painful...
but nothing is as painful
as staying stuck where you don't evolve.

✦

I've realized that if I ever
lost someone
for having too much heart;
for caring too much,
for loving too hard;
for having standards that are too high;
for trying my best to earn
loyalty, love, and respect;
well—the loss was never mine, to begin with.

✦

Maybe it's not about trying to fix something broken.
Perhaps it's about starting over
and creating something better.

✦

The healing process is a minute at a time,
and sometimes you just have to let it hurt.
Hang onto the souls that love you.

✦

Even if you show people your scars,
they will never understand
how much it hurts—
because they only see it
after it heals.

✦

Forgiveness is key.
If you can't learn
to forgive and evolve,
you'll be stuck in a position
that will hold you back forever.

✦

It eventually gets better.
You're no longer angry,
hurt, or bothered by the things
that took so much
of your energy and thoughts.
You will find yourself in a peaceful place.
If not now, then eventually!

✦

I wanted revenge,
but instead,
I found peace.

The broken will always be able
to love harder than most.
Once you have been in the dark,

you're going to appreciate
everything that shines.

✦

Shout out to the pain
that gave me understanding.
And made me
The stronger I have ever been!

✦

Sometimes God has to break you down
to bless you up.
Learn from your mistakes.
Let worry and doubt leave you,
and let God's peace and love fill you.

✦

Those L's weren't losses,
they were lessons you needed
to experience and learn from.

✦

I'm no longer broken—
I'm healing,
I'm rediscovering,
I'm starting over...
This is my rebirth!

✦

Everything happens for a reason.
Keep your intentions pure,
sit back, and watch everything

fall into place—
and the right will reveal,
and your heart will heal.
Hold on!

✦

The most beautiful part about being broken is
when the healing begins.

✦

There comes a time of healing,
no matter how broken you are right now;
No matter how heavy your heart is right now...
you will heal.

✦

If we don't change, we don't grow...
we don't learn...
we won't adapt...
we won't be challenged and refined...
We won't have new opportunities.

✦

If we refuse to change,
we're refusing to get better.
Don't fear change, embrace it.

✦

Sometimes, life closes doors
because it's time to move forward,
and that's good—

because we often won't move
unless circumstances force us to.

pray about it as much you stress about it
pray about it as much you stress about it
pray about it as much you stress about it
pray about it as much you stress about it
pray about it as much you stress about it...

I used to see pain, now I see a purpose.
I used to see hurt, now I see healing.
I used to see loss, now I see love.

Life now makes more sense without a blurry vision.

Chapter 4:

Healing

I'm thankful for all the pain—
All the pain I suffered
was worth all the happiness
I now have;
all the love I have for myself
was way more than you could
ever give me.

I just want to put this out there—
it is okay to be vulnerable.
You can be open and honest
about what's going on
in your heart.
I'm learning now that
this is the only way
I can find healing.

"You yourself, as much as anybody in the entire universe, deserve your love and affection."
– Buddha

Self-love and healing is the way!

To The Ones Who Held Me Down

My Aunty Georgia has been
such a significant part
of my healing—
She has mentored and advised me,
been my guidance and light
in my darkest times—
She has helped me heal
my heart, soul, and mind.

My *Aunty Georgia* is a real gem,
and for this, I am grateful.
She was there for my sister and me,
at home and in the hospital.
I will always remember her words
when she told me
she's my spiritual mother.

I believe
my mom knew she was leaving
and she wanted us to grow closer.

So, I want to take a moment
to thank you, *Aunty Georgia*,
for your love

and your guidance—
And I am grateful
to all the others
who have been there,
even if in silence.
For your mere presence was my strength.

Georgia Welwood, *Janjay Sherman*, *Candice Davies*, and *Jessica Lindsey* – you all have a special place in my heart!

And I know my mom was—and is—still smiling… in the end, and from the start!

JanJay, my dearest sister:

You have been a gem throughout,
always there to catch me when I rise and when I fall.
You never gave up on me,
even when I was at my lowest—
and weakest,
and worst!
And we have been through
so many tests together,
that now I know
our bond is honest.

Your strength and resilience
are truly inspiring,
and your courage and support
have helped profoundly
in my harmonizing.

The same is true for you, *Candice:*
you are like my sister,
although you are my cousin—
A sister from another mother.
I have never met anyone
more genuine, sweet, and loving.

Thank you, *everyone*,
for loving and accepting me.
For your understanding
and being there
in times of need.

Jessica Lindsey, you know
you have been a mother figure,
a best friend,
and a mentor to me.
I would like to thank you
for allowing me
to be a part of your family.
She has supported me
in each and every way possible.
Constantly being a light
in my life
and uplifting me.
I wouldn't be where I am today
if it wasn't for her.
She's truly one of a kind.
An amazing spirit, indeed!

Aunty Georgia, Janjay,
Candice, Jessica,
and everyone who was there
with me in this journey—
You all have significant roles in my life.
Angelic blessings, here to show myself—
and the world—
that their love is truly divine.

Thank you.
From the core of my heart!

You can choose
to come to terms
with the broken pieces...
You can either allow yourself
to ruminate in your pieces
or make peace
with the reality
to move forward.
The choice is always yours...
The decision rests with you!

✦

You can't be
somebody else's peace
if you are dealing with a storm.
How can you give
what you don't have?
It is impossible to pour
from an empty cup.
Take care of yourself first.
Make peace with your past,
be at peace
with who you are;
and pick up the pieces
of your broken heart.

✦

Forget the past.
It keeps you
from enjoying
your present and the future.
Some of life's best lessons are learned
through the worst times.
Hold on.
You will come out
Stronger than ever!

✦

Whoever is reading this,
I pray that you find happiness.
Not temporary happiness—
but long-lasting,
a real pleasure.
I wish you
eternal happiness and bliss.
You deserve it, sis!

✦

You won't find peace
outside of God's presence.
The healing that you are seeking
is found in Him—
not in people or things.

✦

This year taught me
about love, loss, heartbreak,
and strength.
I never could've imagined
this multitude of pain—
but I also could've never imagined
this multitude of triumph.
This year taught me
that my existence does not need
to be rooted in trauma.
It's ok to move on.
It's ok to heal.

✦

Inner peace is a new success.
I hope we all come out
as winners,
one day!

Wholeness

What exactly is healing, anyway?
Life is a journey—
transient and flowing.
Aren't we always on a journey of healing?
Can we ever indeed be 'healed?'

I believe life is cyclic,
like the stars that spin
in the night's sky—
And the moon that shines
silently, protecting the earth
in her warm glow.

"Wholeness does not mean perfection: it means embracing brokenness as an integral part of life."

-Parker J. Palmer

Call me a lunatic if you will,
but I've come to realize,
with sun and the moon,
stars and galaxies,
life has feminine energy—
A power presence...

Healing is wholeness,
and emotions are feminine—
Just like the mind is
masculine, in essence.
Sometimes, true healing only begins
when we become
in tune with our essence,
our divine feminine wisdom,
and emotional sensitivity.
Our intuition and dreams...
the subconscious is real.
Dreams are real,
and so is Spirit.

Healing is the wholeness and unity you see
on the other side of the veil—
where there is no veil.

✦

In happy moments: **Praise** God
In difficult moments: **Seek** God
In quiet moments: **Worship** God
In confusing moments: **Trust** God
In every moment: **Thank** God

✦

This is the last thing
that I want to tell you:
I want you to put yourself first,
no matter who you fall in love with.
I want you to love yourself
like it's the only thing left to do.
You matter!

✦✦

My Story

May 17th, 2016

May 17th is the day that I lost a piece of me. Watching my mother take her last breath in front of me is something that had truly traumatized me and left me scarred for life. Frozen in time and left with nothing but memories of a lifetime. I didn't get any final words from my mom. Nor was I able to say anything. I think we were both in denial. We wanted to have faith and believe that she was going to make it through. That she was going to come back home all healthy and fine.

I remember when they brought her home from the hospital on May 17th —I kept asking her if she would like me to get a notepad for her to write something down. I got this idea because, at this point, she couldn't speak and I thought maybe she would pen down things she wanted to say. In her last moments. But there was so much chaos going on at that time that I forgot.

I regret it every day because she passed away shortly after.

The hardest thing that my father, siblings, and I had to go through was having to sit down and tell my mother that she didn't have to keep holding on and that it was okay. The nurse had told us that her organs were shutting down, but my strong mom was fighting it.

She didn't want to let go. She didn't want to leave us. I didn't want her to leave either, and for some reason even with the nurse saying her organs were shutting down, I still couldn't grasp the fact that my mother was dying.

I remember my sister saying, "*Mommy, it's okay I will take care of NeeJay and Toga...*" Us saying our goodbyes to her in my bedroom was the hardest thing I've ever been through. Everything was happening so fast.

The night before, at the hospital, I was sitting beside her bed telling her that I knew she was going to be okay—and that she was going to live a long life. Shortly after, I went to go sleep in the waiting area—and my dad came in at 6 am, telling me that the doctor said there was nothing more they could do for my mom.

The doctor had told my dad and sister that "God was calling her home."

Fast-forwarding to me, being in my bedroom saying goodbye was unbelievable. Once, we told my mom that it was okay with my aunt saying, "Your beloved is waiting for you (God)..."—And with that, she took her last breath. I burst out of the room, ran up the stairs—running outside, falling to the ground in the middle of the street, screaming, crying as my aunts and cousin held me. That day and those moments still haunt me.

A part of me died that day. Within a timeframe of 10 days of being diagnosed out of the blue, my mother passed away. Life is too short and unpredictable. Cherish your mom today, and every day—and let her know how much she means to you... Life hasn't been the same since I lost my mom, and I know it will never be. She was our everything and more. You only get one mother, and I was blessed with an amazing one.

If you asked me what my expectations have been for the last three years, I would have responded to you optimistically: a year full of new opportunities and prosperity. As the youngest of the three siblings, my dream has always been to be the one in the family to take care of everyone, to make things happen, to change everyone's life. I wanted to be the one to buy my mom her dream home and rid her of debt. I wanted to be the one to change her life and take care of her. As life often goes—the last three years have been full of twists and turns, challenges and pains, and things I never expected.

On March 16th, 2016, I came home from college for spring break to visit my family. During my stay, I went to visit my mom at her new store – House of Jubilee. The store was a second-hand store she had opened, where a portion of the proceeds would help women in need, as part of her ministry.

While at the store that day, my mother and I spent two hours praying that the year would be full of blessings, spiritual growth, and no more struggles. That night, I prayed as I had never prayed before. Every word I spoke—I said it with so much faith, passion and enthusiasm. As I begged, I wanted her to know how much I loved her and appreciated all of the sacrifices she had made for me and or the whole family. Never had I imagined that this time in prayer with my mother was going to be my very last precious, intimate moment with her.

I returned back to New York to finish the last semester of school before summer. Upon my return, I learned that my father was scheduled to have prostate surgery on April 29th, so I planned to go back to Kansas City to be with my family for the procedure.

When I returned home for my father, I learned that my mother had also been admitted to a different hospital for some medical condition. After a few days and several rounds of testing, on May 7th, my mother was diagnosed with stage IV pancreatic cancer. My sister later shared with me that she had been sick for about a month, but they kept this from me to avoid distracting me from completing my semester.

May 16th—the doctors told my family that there was nothing more they could do for my mother. Cancer had spread to her liver and lungs. On May 17th, my mother had lost the battle against cancer. God decided to call my best friend home. She passed away at home in my bedroom, surrounded by family.

***

My mother dedicated her life to teaching me and everyone she met, that with God, all things are possible. She pushed to accomplish something, no matter what the situation may look like. She was born in Liberia, West Africa—and was the oldest girl of a large family. She came to America as a foreign exchange student when she was 18 years old. Later, when the civil war hit Liberia years later—my mother rescued her whole family, bringing them to America—all seven of her siblings, and my grandparents. She was brave and selfless and would give her very last to anyone in need.

My mom was my biggest supporter; my cheerleader, my motivation, my best friend—my everything, and without her, I feel so lost. I shed so many tears while writing this. I had just turned 20 years old on July 1st—and before my mom passed, I felt like I had it all figured out. Now, I don't know what to do. I wake up every day feeling all empty and confused as to why God had to take my mommy away from me—but I know that she wouldn't want me to give up. I am strong – at least I'm trying, and I write this book for her. As a keepsake of the bond we shared and the memories we created while she was alive.

In the end

After my mother's demise, I started running away from God because I blamed him for taking away the most important person in my life.

But in the end, my brokenness led me back to God. Healing and restoration are on the way—and it feels incredible.

Trade-in your broken pieces for God's peace. This is the only way to peace.

About the Author

NeeJay Sherman is passion, emotions, and resilience – personified. A true being of service at heart and soul, NeeJay has seen and endured some of the most heart-breaking incidents, in 23 years of her life. She's smart, educated, and like they say – a perfect combination of beauty and brains! However, what really defines her true being is her unnerving valor, strength of steel, and resilience that wouldn't break.

NeeJay's work entails profound stories of love, loss, grief, healing and self-love. Her poetry bleeds emotions that all humans feel and has a magical power to relate with the reader. Her poetry connects with the reader on a deeper level, sparking suppressed emotions and embarking them on a journey of healing and overcoming the grief. While reading her work, you will find yourself embark on a journey of self-discovery – and you will find strength you never knew you had!

Her poetry lights up your heart, allows you to ache and grieve but also pushes you out of it. And this is what makes her work stand out from her contemporaries.

NeeJay's debut book, *Broken to Peace*, has been written with intentions to inspire and empower others to rise up from their pain and despair, and step up into their light. Although still young, just 23 years of age, NeeJay has already been through so much—and wishes to assist others on their journey to healing and self-love.

NeeJay Sherman is the perfect embodiment of her zodiac sign Cancer, Nurturing, compassionate, sensitive and sincere—with a great love for creativity, family, and her inner feminine intuition. She wants to impact others' lives positively, to provide encouragement, share motivation, and be a guiding light—to remind others to never give up in the face of challenging circumstances and testing times. She believes in the process of wrapping ourselves in the healing energy of love, compassion, and acceptance to get through the pain that we all experience in life.

Neejay grew up in Kansas City, however, she moved to New York city and has been living there for the last five years. She is passionate about holistic living—all things natural, healthy and organic—and the power of positive thinking. Her debut book and all of her other works are meant to be a catalyst for others through genuine connection, inspiring every reader to set off on a journey of self-discovery and achieve their dreams.

The name *NeeJay* is from the Bassa dialect in Liberian language, meaning "*For your sake*," or "*Because of you*." She believes, from the deepest core of her heart, that her name is a part of her purpose—and this reflects in her writings, personal reflections, and poetry.

Broken to Peace was inspired by the passing of her mother—and by her own story, her life path, and the realizations that came to her along the way. The young author believes that every person has a unique role to play in protecting our beautiful planet, through having the courage to chase their dreams and live their best life. That like her mother, we can all be an example of triumph over adversity—through faith in God, visionary drive, and hard work. That we can all epitomize greatness, healthy self-love, heartfelt sacrifice and hope—for the benefit of others, humanity, and Mother Earth.

✧

✧

✧

NeeJay's favorite quote:

"I can do all things through Christ who strengthens me." ~Philippians 4:13

✧

✧

✧

Made in the USA
Middletown, DE
14 May 2020